Manuel Barrueco
THE MUSIC OF ERNESTO LECUONA

CONTENTS

Project Manager: Aaron Stang
Technical Editor: Jack Allen
Engraver: W.R. Music
Photo of Manuel Barrueco: David Thompson
Cover Design: María A. Chenique & Joe Klucar

LA COMPARSA

By ERNESTO LECUONA
Arranged by MANUEL BARRUECO

5

DANZA LUCUMÍ

By ERNESTO LECUONA
Arranged by MANUEL BARRUECO

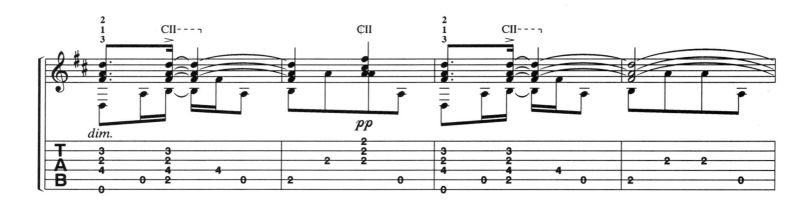

Poco più mosso

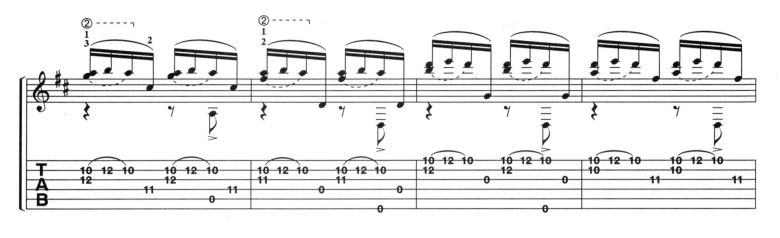

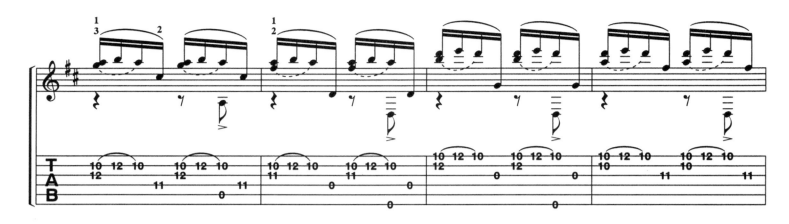

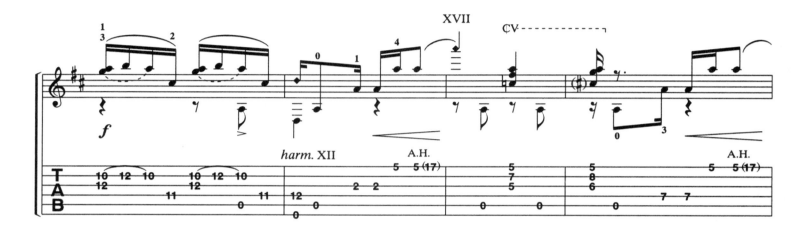

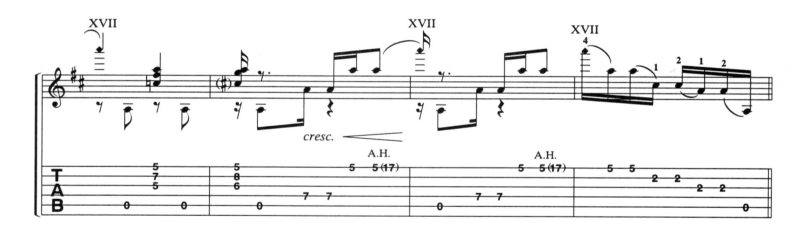

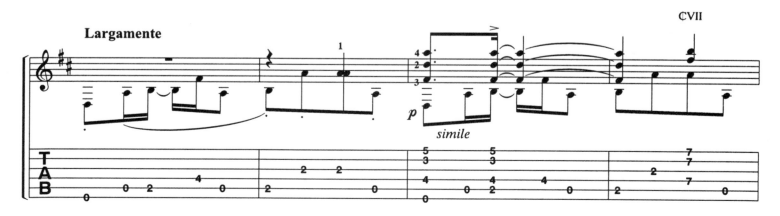

Danza Lucumí - 7 - 6
PGM0004

12

A LA ANTIGUA

By ERNESTO LECUONA
Arranged by MANUEL BARRUECO

About the Music

Ernesto Lecuona was born in Guanabacoa, Cuba, in 1896, and he died in Tenerife, Spain, in 1963. He became internationally famous mostly because of his songs and his piano music.

"Danza Lucumí" and "La Comparsa" form part of his collection of *Afro-Cuban Dances,* which he wrote for the piano. Lucumí refers to the descendants of the Yoruban slaves who came to Cuba from the area around Nigeria in Africa, and "La Comparsa" depicts the coming and going of a dance carried through the streets during carnivals. Also written for the piano, "A la Antigüa" ("In the Old Style") is "Cuban" as opposed to "Afro-Cuban," and as the title suggests it is composed in the style of an earlier Cuba.

Especially in *Afro-Cuban Dances,* it is important to play the rhythmic bass parts completely independent from the singing melodies while always playing behind the beat as though the Cuban heat would slow us down just a bit.

A recorded version of these pieces can be heard in a CD called *¡Cuba!* which I recorded for the EMI label.

Manuel Barrueco